xcxcxc

Jason and the Argonauts

Jason and the *Argonauts*

by Will Osborne
and Mary Pope Osborne

Illustrated by Steve Sullivan

SCHOLASTIC INC.

New York   Toronto   London   Auckland   Sydney

ISBN 0-590-41152-7

Copyright © 1988 by Will Osborne and Mary Pope Osborne.
All rights reserved. Published by Scholastic Inc.
Art direction by Diana Hrisinko.
Text design by Theresa Fitzgerald.

12 11 10 9 8 7 6 5 4 3   8 9/8 0 1 2 3/9

Printed in the U.S.A.   11
First Scholastic printing, February 1988

To Bill and Marjorie Osborne

Introduction

The stories the ancient Greeks told about their gods and heroes are called the Greek myths. One of the most famous is the story of a young hero, Jason, and his quest for the Golden Fleece. Some historians believe this myth might be based on an actual Greek sea voyage that took place around 1300 B.C. But whether the original story was true or not, the tale was a popular one and was passed from generation to generation. Each generation added to the story, and today there are many different versions of Jason's voyage.

All versions, however, tell of the golden ram that saved the life of Jason's ancestor, Phrixus. Years before Jason was born, young Phrixus and his sister Helle were in danger of being murdered by their cruel stepmother.

Hermes, the messenger god of Mount Olympus,

took pity on the children and sent a golden ram to rescue them. The children climbed on the ram's back, and the mighty animal bore them away through the sky. But as they were flying over the sea, Helle fell from the ram's back and drowned. Phrixus traveled on alone to Colchis, a kingdom by the Black Sea.

Phrixus was received kindly by King Aeetes, the fierce ruler of Colchis. To show his gratitude, Phrixus sacrificed the golden ram to the gods and gave the animal's magical golden coat to the king.

King Aeetes hung the ram's fleece in a sacred grove where a sleepless dragon guarded it night and day. This wondrous coat of magical golden wool became known far and wide as the Golden Fleece.

CHAPTER ONE

Return to Iolcus

"Jason."

The young man with the yellow mane of hair stirred but did not open his eyes.

"Jason. It is time to rise."

The rough voice cut sharply into Jason's morning dreams. He opened one eye and squinted at the strange-looking beast who spoke to him from the mouth of the cave. The creature was Chiron the Centaur, half man and half horse.

"Jason. It is almost time to go."

"Yes, yes, I know," murmured Jason, rolling over onto his side. "I'm awake."

Chiron stamped his hooves, and the sound echoed through the cave. "JASON!"

Jason sprang from the cave floor onto his feet. "All right!" he said.

Chiron smiled as Jason stumbled out into the light of the rosy dawn. The young man was one of

Chiron's favorite pupils: strong-willed, athletic, powerful; yet gentle and reasonable, with an easy sense of humor and grace. The perfect combination for a great leader of men.

Jason stretched his lean, muscular body in the sun, then splashed his face with water from the cold mountain stream beside the cave. "When you reach Iolcus today, Jason, remember well what I have taught you," said Chiron. "Keep to the cool path of reason unless you *must* fight, and then. . . ."

" 'Fight with a strong arm and a cool head.' Of course, I remember," Jason said as he pulled on his deerskin tunic.

"And where should you confront your uncle Pelias?" Chiron asked.

Jason smiled. They had been over this many times. "At the festival of the goddess, where all my countrymen might hear," he said, wrapping a leopard skin around his shoulders. "Chiron, I wish. . . ."

"Yes?" said Chiron. "What do you wish?"

Jason gazed down the mountain into the valley below. "I wish you were coming with me."

"No, Jason. This you must do alone. Have I not taught you well enough how to speak with your enemies, how to fight them, and how to know when you should do one and not the other?"

"Yes, but why not come with me today? You are like a father to me."

"You will not need me for a father any more, Jason," Chiron said. "Soon you will find others to help you win back your real father's kingdom."

"But how do you know this?" asked Jason. "How can you be sure I'll find others?"

"Ask me no more questions. Go now. Today is your eighteenth birthday. Today you are a man. Go and seek your throne."

"Father. . . ."

"I am not your father. Go now, Jason."

As Jason made his way down the steep mountain path toward the city of Iolcus, he thought about his childhood with Chiron: the warrior games with the other boys, the lessons in music and poetry, the long evenings by the fire listening to the wise centaur's tales of adventure. As a child Jason had been brought to live in the mountains with Chiron after his wicked uncle Pelias had stolen his father's throne. All his years of training and study had been to prepare him for the day he would return to Iolcus and reclaim his father's kingdom. Many times he had wondered how he would feel when the day finally arrived.

It was almost noon when Jason reached the river at the foot of the mountain. In the distance, beyond the woods, he could hear chariots rattling over the

dusty roads to the city of Iolcus. As he sat on the bank eating the lunch he had brought, Jason could hardly believe that this was really the day he had been anticipating for so long. Why did the meat taste the same? Why did his shoulder still ache from carrying his bronze-bladed spear? Shouldn't everything seem different today?

"Young man! Young man!"

An old woman dressed in rags was calling to Jason from a short distance down the bank. It was odd he hadn't noticed her before.

"Young man, I'm so glad you came along! Will you help me across the river, please?" The old woman slowly made her way up the bank to where Jason sat. "You look so strong! Perhaps you could *carry* me across. Ooh, what pretty hair. . ." she said, running gnarled fingers through Jason's long yellow curls. "Won't you help me, please, pretty man?"

Jason sighed and stood up. The old woman was terribly ugly and her voice grated on Jason's ears, but Chiron had taught him to be courteous and respectful of his elders.

"Yes, I'll carry you across," he said. The old woman squealed and clapped her hands.

The rushing water sparkled in the hot sunlight, and tall reeds swayed and whispered on the muddy banks as Jason hurled his spear to the other side of the water. He held out his arms to the old woman and helped her climb awkwardly onto his back.

"Oh, how lovely," she rasped as the two of them started into the water. "How lovely to be carried by such a handsome, strong young man!"

"Lovely, indeed," gasped Jason. "Are your pockets full of rocks?" The old woman felt heavier than a bag of stones and seemed to get heavier with each step.

"Pockets full of rocks? Oh, no!" the old woman cackled. "Perhaps you are not quite as strong as you look!"

Jason began to wonder if the old woman might be a witch. No human being could be this heavy! "Where do you come from, old woman?" he panted. "Under the earth?"

"No, from heaven, dearie! I come from heaven!"

"Well, you are as heavy as Mount Olympus itself," Jason gasped as he finally heaved her onto the muddy bank on the far side of the river.

• • •

"Oh, dear, look," said the old woman as Jason stepped from the water onto the shore. "I've made you lose one of your pretty sandals!"

Jason looked down at his feet. The old woman was right — his left sandal had been carried off by the rushing water.

"I'm sorry you lost your sandal, Jason." The voice was beautiful and soft. Jason looked up and cried out in surprise. The old woman was gone, and in her place stood the beautiful goddess Hera: wife of Zeus, the mightiest god on Mount Olympus.

"What — where did you come from?" Jason gasped.

Hera smiled. "You are a gentle, strong, beautiful young man, Jason, and your kindness shall not go unrewarded. I know the purpose of your journey today. You are right to seek to reclaim the kingdom of your father. I will travel with you now in spirit, and offer you help and counsel if ever you should need me. I shall help you through your quest as you have carried me across this stream. . . ."

Before Jason could answer, Hera touched his cheek and vanished in a blaze of light.

• • •

The king's messenger ran panting up to the palace gates. "Let me see the king!" he called. "I must see the king immediately! Sire! Sire!" The messenger pushed his way past the palace guards and into the great hall of the palace. "Sire!"

King Pelias heard the shouting in the hall and stepped out of counsel with his advisors.

"I'm sorry for interrupting you, sire," said the messenger, "but this is a matter of the greatest importance! There is a young man at the festival, sire, come down from the mountain. He is so striking, so strong and handsome, some are saying he is a god — or the mortal son of a god! He is creating a disturbance, sire, calling for you. He claims he is your kinsman and the rightful ruler of your kingdom!"

King Pelias dismissed his advisors and called for his guards to accompany him to the festival. As he pushed his way through the crowded streets, he could feel the excitement in the air. This brash young man *was* creating a disturbance, and Pelias feared that the prophecy he had worried about for so long might be coming true.

When Pelias and his guards reached the market-place, the crowd hardly noticed them; all eyes were fixed on the young man in the leopard skin holding the bronze-bladed spear. His golden hair gleamed in the late afternoon sun as he stood proudly in the middle of the square.

But King Pelias was not looking at the young man's hair or his spear or his leopard skin. He was staring at the young man's foot, the foot without the sandal, and his heart was pounding in his chest. Long ago an oracle had warned Pelias to beware of a man wearing only one sandal because that man would take his throne — and his life.

Pelias took a deep breath and tried to smile as

he stepped up to the stranger. "You are welcome in my kingdom, sir," he said graciously. "May we ask why you have favored us with a visit?"

"I am Jason, Uncle, the son of your brother Aeson. I have lived for nearly sixteen years in the mountains with Chiron the Centaur. And now I have returned to claim my father's throne."

Of course, Pelias thought. Jason. The loyal son comes to seek revenge. Well, he is brave, but perhaps he is as foolish as his father. . . .

"Jason," Pelias said softly. "Jason, Jason . . . how you've grown."

Jason stared at Pelias, puzzled by the king's gentle tone. He had expected a much harsher welcome.

"Oh, please, do not worry, my boy. You won't have to fight with me," Pelias said. "I am glad you have come home. In truth, I have long yearned to restore the harmony of our family. Our kingdom has grown and prospered under my rule, Jason, but I am old now and will gladly offer you my place on the throne and all my riches as well."

"Thank you, Uncle," Jason said. "You may keep your riches: your flocks of sheep and herds of cattle. I only wish to rule. . . ."

King Pelias put his arm around Jason's shoulders. "Oh, Jason, let us not worry now about what I shall have or not have. There is another matter that concerns me far more. Come, walk with me awhile, and let me speak with you about it."

The king turned to the crowd and raised his arm. "Go back to your festival," he called. "This man is my nephew, and he is most welcome in our city. Go back to your festival. All is well."

The marketplace began to bustle with activity again as Pelias led Jason away from the square. As they walked, Pelias spoke to Jason like a father. "There is an injustice in our kingdom, Jason, that troubles me deeply. I have hoped for a long time that one such as you would come forward to help me. . . ."

"What injustice, Uncle?" Jason asked.

"You know of the Golden Fleece, Jason? The coat of the golden ram that bore our kinsman Phrixus safely from our land when his life was in danger?"

"I know of the Golden Fleece. But what has that to do with you and me?"

"The Fleece now belongs to King Aeetes of Colchis — an evil, selfish man. Jason, the Fleece should be here! In Iolcus! As a tribute to our kinsman Phrixus, and to the god Hermes who sent the golden ram! I am too old to reclaim this treasure, for the trip to Colchis is arduous and long. But you, *you* could travel to Colchis, Jason, and bring the

Fleece home! I will guard your throne — I would protect it — until you return."

Jason's blood stirred as he listened to Pelias. Chiron had trained him to seek adventure and never to shrink from a challenge; the challenge to capture the Golden Fleece and to restore honor and glory to his new kingdom was tempting indeed.

"I will do it, Uncle!" Jason said. "I will gather the right men to help me. And we will reclaim the coat of the golden ram!"

"Wonderful, Jason!" said King Pelias. "Wonderful! You have made this old man's heart very happy. Now come, let me call for the friends and relatives who have not see you for so many years."

Jason and King Pelias returned to the marketplace. The king sent his messenger to announce Jason's arrival throughout the city, and as the sun set in the distant hills, Jason was reunited with his relatives and the friends of his family amid tears and cries of joy.

Pelias stood alone and watched his handsome nephew laugh and rejoice in the red light of sunset. "Laugh now, Jason," he whispered. "Laugh now. But when you face the horrors of your quest — the rocks that crush all life, the sleepless dragon that guards the Fleece — you will not laugh then, Jason. You will beg for mercy — and curse the day you tried to steal my kingdom!"

CHAPTER TWO
The Argo

ℵ"It cannot be done, my friend! It simply cannot be done!" Argus, master shipbuilder of Greece, threw the rumpled parchment on the tree stump he used for a table.

"Look again," said Jason, picking up the parchment that held his rough sketch of a boat. "I think that with — "

"Oars for fifty sailors?" interrupted Argus, slapping at the plans with his huge hand. "A mast strong enough to bear a thirty-foot sail in high winds? And over how many miles of uncharted ocean? Are you crazy? What about room for your provisions? Food and casks of fresh water for your thirsty sailors? And surely your fifty strong warriors can't sit at their posts and row all day and all night! Where will they sleep?" Argus shook his head. "You see? Your ship grows larger with every question." He turned and stalked toward an ancient oak tree at the top of the hill. "No, my friend," he called over his shoulder. "It cannot be done. It is impossible."

The burly boat builder threw himself down on the grass in the shade of the oak. He drank deeply from a wineskin and watched as his carpenters hewed and shaped a huge timber down by the docks.

Jason leaned against the oak and spoke quietly. "I am sorry to have bothered you, then, Argus. But I was told no challenge could prove too great for your skill. Even the goddesses spoke of you." Argus glanced up at Jason. "You see, I have the blessing of Hera and Athena for this undertaking. . . ."

"Aaah," said Argus. "But what do goddesses know of building ships? What do they know of the difficulties of creating such a . . . a . . ." — he gestured toward Jason's plans — "monstrosity?"

"I quite agree with you," Jason said. "What do the goddesses know of the miracles you would have to perform? They might give this undertaking their blessing, but *you* would have to give it your blood and your skill."

The bushy-bearded man growled in agreement.

"It is for that reason that I would not name the ship after either of the goddesses," said Jason, pulling an oak leaf from the tree.

"Name it?" said Argus. "Who ever heard of naming a ship?"

"No one has ever named a ship before," said Jason. "But when this ship is built, she will be so magnificent she *must* have a name. But I would not name her after the goddesses. I would only name her after you. . . ."

Jason pulled another leaf from the oak and sat down beside the shipbuilder. He held the leaf up to the sun so that it looked like a sail on the sea's horizon. "I can see her clearly," Jason said. "The *Argo*."

Argus stared at the leaf for a moment, then looked down again at his men working by the docks. He took another long drink from his wineskin and scratched his beard. "Well," he growled, holding out his hand to Jason. "Leave me your plans." Jason grinned and handed Argus the folded parchment. Argus stuffed it in his tunic, then gazed back down at the dock. "Perhaps with the proper timbers it might be possible," he said quietly. "We'll see . . . we'll see. . . ."

. . .

It took Argus and his men nearly a year to build Jason's ship. They cut fresh pine for the galley and oak for the oars, and hauled the timbers down to the shore in ox-drawn carts. They steamed the wooden planks with boiling sea water to make them flexible, then shaped them carefully around a strong frame to form a smooth, graceful hull. All the boards were held together with oaken pegs, and the hull was painted with many coats of hot resin to make it waterproof. The trunk of a whole tree was used for the mast, and finally the men sewed and rigged a thirty-foot sail of coarse linen.

By the time the *Argo* was completed, Argus had grown to love the ship so much that he could not bear to let her sail away without him.

• • •

"Even Argus is sailing with Jason on his voyage for the Golden Fleece," said Hylas, Hercules' young arms bearer. Hylas was preparing dinner for Hercules at their campsite in the woods. "It seems all of Greece wants to sail with him."

"All of Greece, eh?" Hercules laughed. "Tell me more, Hylas. Just who exactly is 'all of Greece'?"

"Well, it is said that Theseus and Nestor have joined him, and Calais and Zetes. . . ."

"Zetes and Calais?" said Hercules. "The sons of the North Wind?"

"Yes!" said Hylas, handing Hercules a bowl of stew. "And Euphemus, the fastest runner in all the world! I have heard he can run across water without wetting his feet."

"Humph," said Hercules. "Do not believe everything you hear. Who else?"

"Castor, the finest horseman in the land; and his twin, Pollux, the best boxer; and Tiphys, the greatest seaman! He can tell from the sun and stars when a storm is coming. . . ."

"I can tell from the rain in my face when the storm has arrived," Hercules muttered, his mouth full of stew. "Does that make me a great sailor, too?"

"And Orpheus will be traveling with them. . . ."

"Orpheus?" sputtered Hercules. "Orpheus is no great warrior!"

"I know, but he is the greatest musician in all Greece. He has offered his songs and the music of his lyre to inspire the sailors and help win the favor of the gods! And Athena has offered her sacred blessing for the journey, and. . . ."

"Enough!" roared Hercules. "It seems, doesn't it, that the only name missing is mine! Prepare for a journey, Hylas. We will complete Jason's list of heroes by offering him the services of the most powerful man on earth!"

And so, on a cool, clear morning eleven months after Pelias issued his devious challenge, fifty of Greece's greatest heroes assembled at the port of Iolcus to assist Jason in his quest. Hundreds of people from all over Greece gathered by the shore that morning to watch the amazing ship embark.

Even Chiron the Centaur came down from his mountain retreat to see the heroes off.

The celebration began at dawn with a great breakfast feast for the heroes and the crowd alike. After the feast, the fifty sailors, whom Jason called the *Argonauts*, encircled the ship with a stout rope. A cheer rose from the crowd as they realized the moment of departure was finally at hand.

The Argonauts tipped the ship onto the smooth wooden rollers they had placed in her path to the sea. At Argus' signal the men all pushed, and the *Argo* began to make her way toward the bay. The great ship moved slowly and heavily at first, but as she picked up speed the rollers began to smoke, and the Argonauts had to haul hard on the rope to keep her from crashing too soon into the water.

The *Argo* splashed into the bay, and her huge mast rocked sharply to the left and then the right. The crowd roared as the great ship finally settled upright in the water, the mast pointing toward the heavens.

Once all the Argonauts were aboard, Jason climbed up the mast to address the crowd on the shore.

"My friends," Jason shouted, "my heart swells with pride to see you all here today. And I must thank the gods forevermore for sending this noble, heroic group of men to aid me in my quest for the Golden Fleece."

Jason gestured toward the heroes on the deck of the *Argo*, and the crowd cheered. Then Jason held up his hands for silence and called toward the heavens.

"Hear me, Hera! Remember your promise to be my guide! Athena, send us your strength and courage, for our journey is long and treacherous! Hear me, Apollo! Steer us by the sun and wind! And hear me, Poseidon! Tame the waters of your great ocean so that the sea may always be our friend and never our enemy!"

As Jason offered his prayer to Poseidon, Tiphys handed him a golden goblet full of wine. The crowd and the heroes were silent as Jason poured the wine into the sea, a special offering to the great god of the ocean.

No one made a sound as the heroes took their places at the oars. As the *Argo* rocked gently in the calm waters, Orpheus began to play his lyre; and the soft, sweet melody drifted over the crowd and up to the heavens themselves. Then from the west a great wind began to blow, and the quiet was broken by Jason's call: "Haul up the sail!"

The *Argo*'s great sail billowed in the wind, and the Argonauts pulled on their oars. The men began shouting and cheering as they rowed, and the roar of the crowd was almost deafening as the magnificent ship skated across the sunlit water out to sea.

The Argonauts soon settled into a comfortable routine on board the ship. Orpheus set the pace for the oarsmen with his lyre: When the wind was low, his rhythms were hard and driving, spurring them on; when the wind was up, the music was sweet and flowing, giving the oarsmen a chance to rest their arms and backs.

The first leg of their journey carried the Argonauts along the Grecian coast. Each day as the sun began to set, eagle-eyed Lynceus, the lookout, would find a suitable inlet along the shore where the *Argo* could be safely moored. Evenings were filled with stories of each hero's adventures, and the *Argo* would embark again at dawn, the men rested and refreshed.

When the Argonauts reached the foot of Mount Athos, they could no longer follow the Grecian coastline and had to put out to the open sea. They loaded the ship with all the provisions they could carry and set sail for the remote island of Lemnos, an isolated land that enjoyed little contact with the outside world. Lemnos was to be their first stop on the long journey to Colchis, and Jason wondered if the people of the island would receive the travelers as friends or as enemies. He remembered Chiron's counsel: Count no man your enemy until he has refused to be your friend.

But nothing Chiron had taught him could prepare Jason for what he was about to encounter on the island of Lemnos.

CHAPTER THREE

Hercules

✍"Hylas, can you see? Are they still there?" Mighty Hercules was pacing up and down the deck of the *Argo* as Hylas looked out over the sea from the mast.

"No, I see no one, but there is smoke from the chimneys. . . . Wait. . . . Yes! I hear Orpheus' lyre . . . and the sounds of a feast, I think."

"Feasting again? Enough! We can wait no longer!"

Hercules grabbed his huge club and jumped over the side of the ship into the cold water. He was furious with his shipmates. As he waded angrily ashore, he wondered what strange powers the Lemnian women could possess that would so easily disarm such a great collection of heroes.

Jason might have wondered, too, had he not been so completely under the spell of Queen Hypsipyle's charms. When the *Argo* had landed on the island, the men were welcomed ashore by the queen and a group of powerful women in suits of armor. Jason was surprised to learn that there were no men on the island at all. It seems that long ago the women had risen up in anger against their cruel husbands and killed them and all their male children as well. Now, after many years of isolation, the women were so happy to see the men of the *Argo* that they welcomed them eagerly into their village and their homes, feasted them with good wine and excellent food, and showed them such loving hospitality that even Jason was tempted to abandon his quest and live out his days peacefully with the queen.

Only Hercules and his companion Hylas had returned to the ship and had not been tempted by the Lemnian women. Now, as Hercules strode wet and angry through the village, it was clear that his frustration with his shipmates had reached its peak.

"Come out, men of Greece! Return to your ship and your journey!" Hercules banged his club against the door of the banquet hall. "Come out and face the sea again!"

Hercules' only answer was the sound of the banquet inside. Furious, he kicked down the door and strode through the hall, swinging his club. "Get back to your ship! The feasting is over!" he boomed to the lounging heroes. "Get up!"

A few of the Argonauts struggled to their feet;

a few called to Hercules to join them at the table; but most ignored him completely.

Hercules crashed his club against the walls and roared for the men to move — or he'd kill them.

The women began to yell at Hercules to go away and mind his own business, but this only enraged the mighty warrior more. He started hauling the Argonauts bodily from the hall, carrying two and sometimes three at a time out the door and into the street. "Get back to the ship!" he roared. "Get back to the ship, or I'll kill you all!"

. . .

When the last man had been dragged out of the hall, Hercules turned to the astonished women. "Where is Jason? Where is the man we once looked to as leader?" he demanded.

One of the women pointed to a room off the main hall: Queen Hypsipyle's private dining chamber. Hercules grunted and stormed up to the door. He gave it a mighty kick, and the door swung open to reveal Jason and the beautiful queen.

"What are you doing?" bellowed Hercules. "Why are you ignoring your duty to your men and your quest?"

"I have a new duty," Jason replied sleepily. "Queen Hypsipyle has asked me to stay and rule this island with her." Hypsipyle poured more wine into Jason's silver goblet. "I am to be her king. . . ."

Hercules snatched the goblet and threw the wine in Jason's face. "This is not your destiny!" he bellowed. "Our quest is for the Golden Fleece! You will have a kingdom to rule, with honor and glory; but a kingdom you must win, not be handed on a silver platter!" Hercules grabbed Jason's shoulders and stared deeply into his eyes. "No one, *no one,* has ever undertaken such a quest as ours, and *nothing* must delay us or dim the burning vision of what we seek!"

Jason seemed to wake from a dream. He shook his head and looked around him, a confused expression on his face. "Yes," he said. "Yes, I know. . . . I . . . I had lost my vision. . . . I. . . ." He pulled himself away from Hypsipyle. "I'm sorry," he said to her. "I must leave you. I had almost forgotten. . . ."

Hypsipyle reached for Jason's arm. "No," she whispered. "Please stay. You will be happy here. I will make you happy."

"No," said Jason. "I must get back to my ship." He took her hands in his. "But I will come back," he said, kissing her fingers. "I will come back soon, I promise. . . ."

Hercules grabbed Jason and shoved him out the door. "No, he won't!" he called over his shoulder. "At least, not soon!"

And so the Argonauts continued on their journey, but Hercules remained angry and sullen. He insisted that the men row all day and all night to make up for the time they had wasted on Lemnos.

As the days wore on, the skies and the sea grew calmer, until one morning there seemed to be no wind at all. The sail of the *Argo* hung limply in the early sun. Without the help of the wind, the ship moved slowly and heavily through the sea, and the oarsmen began to grow weary at their posts. Orpheus sang and played his lyre to keep them rowing, but in the still, hot morning, even his music sounded tired.

Only Hercules was undaunted. From his oar at the stern of the ship, he began to taunt his shipmates.

"It seems that I made a mistake, Hylas," he called, loud enough for all to hear. "I must have left the heroes on Lemnos and taken the women by mistake."

No one laughed at Hercules' joke. Hercules nodded at Jason, who was struggling not to show his fatigue. "Look at that, Hylas," Hercules said. "No real man would be so tired this early in the day. Maybe one of us is better suited to commanding a banquet table than a ship!"

Jason said nothing. He gritted his teeth and pulled harder on his oar.

"Hylas," called Hercules, "did you not tell me that Jason had assembled men of great strength for his quest? What did you call them? Heroes? Where are they, Hylas? Where are the heroes?"

"They are here, Hercules," said Jason, hauling hard on his oar.

"Are they?" said Hercules. "Funny, I didn't notice any 'heroes' here. . . ."

"Perhaps you didn't notice them," panted Jason, "because you were making too much noise with your mouth."

"Indeed," growled Hercules. "Well, if there are heroes here, let them hear my challenge: If any man here can outlast me at his oar, I will shut my mouth, after I have called that man my master and lord."

No one spoke a word, but it was soon obvious that all the Argonauts had accepted Hercules' challenge. Each man leaned into his oar with new strength, and the ship surged forward in the water. Orpheus played a lively tune on his lyre and suddenly the ship had the feeling of one of the great Olympic games.

But every man's strength has its limit, and one by one the oarsmen fell from the competition, until only Castor, Pollux, Jason, and Hercules remained. Finally Castor cried out that he could go on no longer, and as he dropped his oar, his twin, Pollux, did the same, leaving the contest to Jason and Hercules alone.

Hercules looked over at Jason and a smile crossed his face for the first time in many days, for this was the competition he had truly been seeking with his taunts. Jason returned the smile and pulled mightily on his oar, causing the ship to veer sharply and jostle Hercules in his seat. Hercules threw back his head and roared, and the two powerful men threw themselves fully into their sport.

The Argonauts cheered both their captain and Hercules on as the two rowed furiously under the hot sun. Jason surprised Hercules with his endurance and determination; the young leader matched him stroke for stroke until the strong man himself was gasping for breath. The two exchanged a look, each recognizing the other's exhaustion, and at last the angry tension between them was broken. Hercules began to laugh, and soon Jason was laughing, too. The rest of the men joined in the laughter as the two sweating, panting contestants lifted and pulled on their oars time after time.

Finally Jason's oar slipped from his hands and the young warrior collapsed on the deck. Hercules shouted and pulled mightily on his own oar; but as he did, the oar snapped in two, sending Hercules sprawling. The great man looked stupidly at the splintered handle in his hands, then hurled it into the sea with a great roar. The men clapped and cheered as he collapsed beside Jason on the deck.

"You have won, my friend," gasped Jason. "I congratulate you."

"No, captain," Hercules panted, "the sea has won, as she always does. She has broken my oar . . . and both our backs as well, eh?"

All the men laughed heartily, then Hercules called to Hylas. "Help me up, boy! And bring a barrel of water for me and my wheezing friend!"

"And Argus must carve you a new oar from stronger wood," said Jason. "Take your posts, sailors!" he called to the rested Argonauts. "We must find this oarsman a mighty tree to match his mighty arms!"

As the other Argonauts threw themselves into their rowing, Jason and Hercules drank deeply from the water Hylas brought. Tiphys steered the *Argo* toward a wooded island barely visible on the distant horizon. They reached the island in the late afternoon, and while the ship was being anchored offshore, Hercules sent Hylas in search of fresh water, and trundled happily off into the forest to find a suitable tree for his new oar.

Hylas laughed as he filled the water jugs at the gurgling spring. He could hear Hercules' bellowing voice in the distance struggling bravely with the melody of the song Orpheus had sung during the contest. Hercules' off-key singing was so loud, Hylas could hardly hear the sounds of the splashing fountain.

It was nearly twilight when Hylas filled the last jug and prepared to return to the ship. A thin moon already hung above the trees of the cool forest glade, and the sound of Hercules' voice had grown more distant. Birds began to give their evening calls, and leaves rustled gently in the breeze. Hylas gathered up his jugs and turned to go.

"Hylaaas. . . ." Hylas thought he heard a sweet voice whisper his name. It must be the leaves rustling in the trees, he thought, or perhaps another bird beginning to sing.

"Hylaaas. . . ." Hylas turned back to the spring. The voice seemed to be coming from the water. It must be the gurgling of the fountain, he thought, or perhaps a turtle splashing into the pond.

"Hylaaas. . . ." The whispery voice was more distinct this time. Hylas was puzzled. The voice was definitely calling his name. Could one of the men from the ship be playing a joke?

Hylas set down his water jugs. He knelt by the pool and peered down at his reflection. As he stared at his shimmering image in the water, another face seemed to take form beneath his own. Hylas found himself peering *through* his own reflection into a softer face, more pale and tender: the face of a beautiful young girl.

Suddenly the image of the two faces was shattered as Dryope, the beautiful water nymph, splashed through the calm surface of the pool. Before Hylas realized what was happening, the lovely creature threw her arms around his neck and pulled him down into the water. "Don't be afraid, Hylas, you beautiful boy," she whispered in his ear. "I love you."

The nymph carried Hylas to the very bottom of the spring, into a grotto filled with beautiful coral and fish and shells. There were other water nymphs there, and they all begged Hylas to stay with them; and the young man, forgetting completely about Hercules and the world he'd left behind, promised that he would.

The surface of the pool was calm again as Hercules tramped through the forest, calling out for Hylas. The great man had uprooted a gigantic fir and was ready to return to the ship.

"Hylas?" Hercules called. "Where are you?"

But Hylas didn't answer. Only the sounds of the birds' songs and the ocean waves broke the silence.

"Hylas? Don't play games with me now, boy!" Hercules shouted. "Answer me! Where are you?"

Hercules stormed into the forest glade and stopped short when he saw Hylas' water jugs beside the pool. Floating on top of the water was the silken band that Hylas often wore about his head. Hercules stared for a moment at the pool; then, thinking that Hylas had drowned, he threw down his club and raised such a cry that the earth shook, the trees trembled, and even the forest spring seemed to be weeping with him in his grief.

Hearing Hercules' cry, Jason and the others ran to the clearing; and though they each tried hard to comfort him, the great man would not be consoled. For hours he sat beside the pool, clutching Hylas' headband to his chest and rocking back and forth. All night long the Argonauts could hear him grieving in the dark forest glade, calling for his friend.

At dawn, a strong wind swept over the wooded island and whipped up the seas. The Argonauts knew they must leave soon to take advantage of the good sailing weather.

Jason tried to persuade Hercules to leave the forest, but Hercules would not budge. So finally, after much debate, Jason was forced to leave the mighty Hercules behind.

As the Argonauts set sail for Colchis, it saddened them all to hear the grieving man's voice still ringing out across the sea. Again and again from deep in the forest, they heard his pained cry: "Hylas! Hylaaas. . . ."

CHAPTER FOUR

The Harpies

꧁"Jason, we should reach Salmydessus by midday," said Tiphys.

Jason didn't answer. He was sitting in the bow of the *Argo*, staring out at the sea. The wind was up, and Orpheus was singing a soft, plaintive song. Jason seemed unaware that Tiphys was speaking to him.

"Captain?" Tiphys said, touching Jason's shoulder.

Jason jumped. "Yes, yes?" he said, turning to Tiphys. "What is it?"

"We're less than a half-day's sailing from Salmydessus," said Tiphys. "Do you still wish to put in there for the night?"

"Oh. Yes," said Jason, getting to his feet. "Tell the men to prepare to land."

Tiphys made his way back to the stern, calling

the landing orders to the men. Jason turned and gazed out at the sea again. He wondered what wise Phineus, the blind prophet king of Salmydessus, would have to say to him.

Jason sighed. Since leaving Hercules on the island, he had fallen deeper and deeper into melancholy. His greatest warrior was lost to him before he had even reached the Colchis shore. At the time, some of the men had called for Jason to go back for Hercules; now, the great warrior's absence weighed heavily on them all. Jason suspected some would even be happy to turn back altogether and abandon the quest.

Jason wondered if Phineus might tell him to give up and return to Iolcus. Perhaps his great quest was merely the folly of a rash young man. But Hera had promised to guide him, and Athena had given her blessing. And hadn't Poseidon sent the West Wind to launch them on their way and spared them thus far from the storms and squalls that all had feared?

No, Jason thought, he would not ask King Phineus *if* he should go on, but *how*. And since Apollo had given Phineus the gift of unfailing prophecy, Jason knew the old king's counsel would be correct.

Jason and his men were met at the palace gates

by Phineus' chief minister. "Greetings, gentle warriors," the minister said, bowing to Jason. "You are most welcome to our lands."

"Many thanks, sir," said Jason, returning the bow. "I have come to request an audience with your king. We have sailed many miles from Iolcus — "

"Oh, yes, yes, I know!" said the minister. "The king has been expecting you!"

Of course, Jason thought, remembering that Phineus could see quite clearly into the future. I wonder if he knows the purpose of my visit as well. . . .

"Follow me," the minister said, ushering Jason and his men into the courtyard. "The king is about to be served his midday meal."

Jason stopped. "Excuse me, sir, but we do not wish to disturb the king while he is dining," he said. "Perhaps we should wait until — "

"Oh, no!" interrupted the minister. "No, no, no!" He leaned in close to Jason and spoke in an ominous tone. "It is important that you see. . . ."

The minister led Jason and the men to the entrance of the king's banquet hall. He held up his hand, signaling them to wait while he peeked through the crack between the two huge oaken doors. Then, heaving a sigh, he pushed open the doors and motioned the men inside.

Jason had expected to find a lavish banquet taking place. Instead, he was shocked to see the old king sitting alone at a huge, empty table on the far side of the hall. The king looked terrible. His body seemed to be nothing but bones. Jason had never seen a living man so thin; surely the king must be suffering from a terrible disease.

Suddenly there was a clattering behind Jason, and a servant wheeling a silver cart pushed past him into the hall. On the cart was a large, covered platter. As the servant scurried nervously up to the king's table, Jason puzzled over the oddness of the event. Why was the sick, blind king dining alone? Where were his attendants and the other members of the court? And why was the servant acting so strangely?

Jason and the men watched as the servant gingerly placed the covered platter before the king. The servant was constantly glancing over his shoulder, looking with terror toward the windows. With trembling hands he lifted the cover from the platter, then raced from the hall, covering his head.

King Phineus reached his bony fingers toward the food that had been placed before him. He gently broke off a tiny crust of bread, but as he lifted it toward his lips, a terrible screeching echoed through the hall, and the room was filled with a horribly foul smell. The king screamed in terror as a swarm of hideous winged creatures swooped down onto the table and snatched the bread from his hand.

Jason and his men watched in stunned silence as the creatures picked through Phineus' dinner with their crooked beaks. Most of what they put in their mouths, they spat out again, and soon the king's meal was spattered all over the table, the walls, and even the king himself. What remained on the platter the awful creatures fouled with their droppings; then they swooped out the windows again, leaving the king with his head in his hands, weeping.

Jason was speechless. He had never seen such a loathsome sight. A team of servants trooped into the hall and began cleaning up the mess, and the minister led Jason and his party up to the king.

"Your Majesty," said the minister, "the Argonauts have arrived."

The old king lifted his head and cried out in relief. "Thank heavens you've come at last," he breathed, his voice weak and trembling. "Please, let us go from this awful place. Guards!"

The old king was too weak even to stand up by himself. The royal guards lifted him from his seat at the table and placed him gently onto a stretcher, then carried him from the hall. Jason and his men followed behind them, relieved to finally get away from the terrible smell.

"My friends, let me tell you now the sad story that lies behind the horrible scene you witnessed today."

The king was lying on his bed in the royal chamber, his head propped up on satin pillows. His voice was weak and thin, and his blind eyes stared vacantly up at the ceiling.

"Since boyhood I have enjoyed the gift of prophecy," Phineus said. "But I have always been careful to use my power wisely and to avoid the many temptations that present themselves to one who can see the future. Even so, my gift itself seemed to anger the great god Zeus. As I grew older, Zeus became more and more jealous of my powers. He claimed that only the most powerful gods on Mount Olympus should be able to look so clearly into the future, and in a fit of rage, he took away my sight."

The old king paused to catch his breath, then continued. "But even my blindness did not satisfy Zeus' anger, and now he sends these Harpies to steal my food and make it impossible for me to eat. For months I have tried to feed my withered body, but to no avail. And now, I fear I am close to death."

The king's minister nodded gravely as Phineus again paused to catch his breath.

"But recently," the king continued, "recently I have seen a vision. I have seen my deliverance coming

44

from the sea in the form of two of your warriors. Jason, my son" — the king reached out for Jason's hand — "Jason, if you will stay and help free me from this curse, I will look deep into my heart and tell you all I can to aid you in your quest."

Jason was very moved by the aged king. He squeezed the old man's bony fingers gently in his own strong hand and spoke softly.

"Sire, after what I have seen today, I would help you whether you could aid us in our quest or not. Let me retire now with my men to make a plan. Tomorrow we shall put it into action."

. . .

The next morning the scene in the banquet hall was the same as it had been the day before. King Phineus sat alone at the long table. The Argonauts watched from their places by the doors as the trembling servant wheeled in his cart, set the food before the blind king, then hurried away with his hands over his head.

The king reached for a crust of bread, and again the sound of screeching and beating wings filled the air as the loathsome Harpies zoomed in through the windows. But just as the horrible creatures swooped down on the king, two of Jason's men, Zetes and Calais, sprang from beneath the banquet table brandishing their swords and shouting at the birds.

The Harpies zoomed back toward the windows, but kicking their winged heels in the air, Zetes and Calais took off after them. And because their father was the North Wind, the two winged Argonauts could fly faster than birds, faster even than the bird monsters sent by Zeus to do his evil bidding.

Zetes and Calais chased the Harpies high into the sky and would have hacked the monsters to pieces with their swords had not Iris, goddess of the rainbow, stopped them.

"Stop! You must not kill the Harpies," Iris commanded the warriors. "They are the hounds of Zeus, the most powerful god on Olympus."

"Then you must forbid these wretched creatures to bother King Phineus ever again," demanded the warriors, "or we will slice them to pieces here and now."

"You have my word; I swear by the River Styx," promised Iris. "Zeus' hounds will never enter Phineus' kingdom again."

• • •

A great cheer arose from the Argonauts as Zetes and Calais returned to the palace. Fresh food was brought for the king, and Phineus wept for joy as he devoured his first meal in many months. The servants brought more food, and all the Argonauts joined the king in his feast. As the banquet drew to a close, Phineus called Jason to his place at the table.

"I am deeply grateful to you, my son, and to your brave men," said the old king. "You have put aside your own concerns to rescue a sick old man from death. But I know your heart is still troubled about your quest."

Jason nodded.

"Come to my chamber at midnight, then, my son," said the king, "and I will tell you all I can. . . ."

CHAPTER FIVE

The Clashing Rocks

✂︎Phineus' chamber was dark except for the gentle glow of moonlight from the window. As the pungent smoke rose from the incense burning at his feet, the king began to speak in a deep, raspy voice: "You have traveled far, my son, and the challenge you face is great. Many dangers still await you."

Phineus warned Jason about the storms and rough seas he was still to encounter. "But the greatest danger by far," said the old man, "lies at the entrance to the Black Sea: the Clashing Rocks of the Bosphorus.

"No ship has ever passed safely between these two giant cliffs, for they are not fixed to the ocean floor. They guard the passage like evil sentries, crashing together and crushing to death any living thing foolish enough to dare passing between them.

"I cannot say whether you shall be able to defy

the cliffs and pass safely through the treacherous channel; that is a test you must face without the aid of prophecy. But I will tell you this: You shall not be the first to pass safely through. There must be one before you, or surely you will all die in the attempt.

"Take with you a mourning dove from my aviary. As you approach the monstrous cliffs, release the dove and bid her seek safe passage. If she fails, you are doomed.

"But if the dove flies safely through the channel, then grip your oars and row with all your might. For I assure you, once you begin, your salvation will come not from your prayers or my prophecies, but from the strength of your arms."

Dawn was breaking outside the palace as Phineus finished his prophecy, and the old king was bathed in the rose-colored light as he spoke his final words.

"Jason, my son, if you do make it through the deadly Clashing Rocks, then you need fear nothing, nothing. . . ."

. . .

Now the terrible test was almost at hand. It was when the wind died down that Jason first heard the sound. On another morning he might have mistaken it for thunder or the surf pounding against a distant shore. Orpheus must have heard it, too, for he stopped his song and gazed out across the rough waters. The oarsmen paused to listen as well, and the ship drifted for a moment in the choppy sea.

Euphemus sat in the bow, stroking the tiny white dove. "Be swift, little bird," he whispered. "You must fly for us like a little eagle."

Jason nodded to Orpheus to continue. The musician resumed his song, and the oarsmen rowed on with grim determination toward the sound of the crashing rocks. Though no one spoke, Jason knew all were thinking of Phineus' ominous words the night before.

As the *Argo* drew closer to the channel, the rumbling and crashing grew louder and louder until it was all the Argonauts could hear. Finally the ship came within sight of the huge granite monsters, and the men were almost overcome with dread. The Clashing Rocks were as formidable a sight as any had ever seen.

Wrapped in a thick mist, the rugged cliffs formed a solid rock wall that completely blocked the channel. Jason called to the oarsmen to hold, and the Argonauts watched in awe as a crack began to appear in the stony facade. With vicious force, the wall began to split itself apart, churning the sea in its wake. When the two halves had separated fully, they crashed together again so swiftly and violently that safe passage through the channel seemed impossible.

Jason was shaken by the display. Nevertheless, he called to Tiphys to hold the ship steady on her course and to Euphemus to be ready to release the dove as soon as the great rocks retreated to their widest point.

But then an idea struck Jason. If the dove were to *begin* her flight *before* the rocks opened, she might gain the precious time needed to make it safely through.

"Hold!" he called, raising his arm to Euphemus. "Wait . . . wait . . . wait. . . ." Jason watched as the great rocks opened to their widest point, then began to rush in again. They met with a thunderous crash and the moment they began to separate, Jason called, "Now!"

Euphemus tossed the dove into the air, and as she shot forward toward the widening gap between the rocks, it looked as if Jason's plan might work and she would make it through. But suddenly the rocks changed direction and crashed in upon one another again, colliding thunderously like two dark monsters. Jason and his men were certain the little bird had been crushed.

But then Euphemus pointed to the sky above the cliffs and shouted, "Look!" and Jason saw the dove flutter up above the treacherous rocks. She had flown between them and come out the other side;

now she was flying high above the foggy mist, silhouetted against the sun.

"Play, Orpheus!" Jason shouted as the dove returned safely to the cheering men. Only a single one of her tailfeathers was missing. "And men, prepare to row as you have never rowed before!"

Orpheus began to play his lyre, and the instant the rocks began to open, Jason called the order to begin rowing. He knew it was a race against time; the *Argo* had to be at least partway through the narrow passage before the rocks changed direction and began to crash together again, or she would never make it.

The ship surged forward, rolling from side to side in the turbulent sea. "Hold her steady, Tiphys!" Jason called. "Use all your might to keep her on course!"

Salt spray drenched the men as the *Argo* began the journey between the rocks. She was more than halfway through the passage when the rocks changed direction and began to close in.

A backwash of huge waves crashed over the *Argo* from either side, and the ship's galley filled with water. Jason called for the strongest oarsmen to stay at their posts and dispatched the others to bail out the galley. But as the rocks continued to close in, the force of the undercurrent became so great that the progress of the *Argo* through the passage slowed to a standstill. Jason called for all the oarsmen to return to their posts. Though they pulled on their oars with all their strength, the *Argo* moved neither forward nor back, but remained squarely in the path of the onrushing rock walls. And each man saw in the rocks his own death, for there seemed no escape from their furious attack.

Then suddenly the crashing surf was silent, and the *Argo* was showered in a blinding golden light. The men let go of their oars and shielded their eyes; Jason looked up into the face of Athena.

The great goddess held the rocks apart with one hand, and with the other, she gave the *Argo* a push that moved the ship safely through the passage.

Athena then vanished as quickly as she had appeared, and the crashing rocks continued on their deadly path. But with Athena's help, the *Argo* was saved; only her stern ornament was lost as the granite monsters crashed together behind her.

The men found themselves safe at last and shouted praises to the great goddess for saving their lives.

Jason looked back at the huge cliffs towering above the ship, then turned to the men. "My friends," he called, "it seems Athena has spared all our lives so that I might continue in my quest for the Fleece. I am thankful to her; but I am also thankful to you for your faith and your bravery. You have offered up your lives for this quest, and I will be forever grateful."

All the men cheered Jason and swore their allegiance to him and to the success of the quest. Then Orpheus began to play, and the Argonauts rowed on, certain that nothing could stop them now.

CHAPTER SIX

Medea

⚹Hera lifted the pitcher from the marble table and filled Athena's goblet. "Holding back the rocks was timely," she said to her stepdaughter. "I don't think they would have made it through without your help."

"Jason and his men are quite able," Athena said quietly. "If I hadn't helped them, they might well have saved themselves." The gray-eyed goddess raised the goblet to her lips. Her mighty spear and shield glistened beside her in the sunlight of Hera's Olympian garden.

"Perhaps," said Hera. "But I suspect they will need us more than ever once they reach Colchis. Do you really think Aeetes will let them walk into his kingdom and take the Fleece without a fight? Look."

Hera set the silver pitcher on the ground, then closed her eyes and waved her hand over the tabletop.

The hard marble surface dissolved into a gray vapor, and Athena watched intently as a scene began to take form beneath the swirling mist. The setting was a stretch of beach along the Colchis coast and as the mist cleared, Athena could make out the band of Argonauts silently mooring the *Argo* among the reeds. In the distance rose the towers of King Aeetes' palace, their golden turrets gleaming in the late afternoon sun.

"How splendid they all look," whispered Athena as she and Hera watched the men struggle to haul the ship ashore. "How brave and handsome. . . ."

"Yes," said Hera. "But I'm afraid their enemy is more formidable than they know. . . ."

Hera passed her hand over the table again, and the scene changed to the courtyard inside the royal palace. The king's troops were assembled before him, and the king was gruffly shouting orders to one of his commanders.

"You see?" Hera said. "I fear even our collection of heroes may be no match for a king's standing army."

"What can we do?" asked Athena.

Hera smiled mysteriously. "Wait," she said, and again she passed her hand over the table. This time when the mist cleared, it revealed another part of the king's palace: a bedchamber, and on the bed was a beautiful young woman. The woman was studying a small black book. Five red candles burned in a circle at her feet.

"Medea?" exclaimed Athena.

"Yes," said Hera. "The king's sorceress daughter. Her magic is strong indeed. . . ."

"But she is fiercely loyal to her father!" said Athena. "What use is she to us?"

"There are other loyalties in the world," said Hera, smiling. "And the loyalty of two lovers can be very powerful indeed." Hera rose from her chair. "Come, stepdaughter," she said, "let us pay a visit to Aphrodite, the goddess of love."

The two goddesses rose and started to leave the garden, but Hera stopped. "Just a moment," she said, turning back to the table. She passed her hand over the surface, and the scene changed once again to the Argonauts as they made their way through the woods toward the city. "Perhaps this will aid their passage through the streets," Hera said. She began to move her hand in a circle over the table, and as she did, a thick mist descended over the scene. "Travel safely, brave heroes," she said, then turned and followed Athena out of the garden.

• • •

Jason and his men were surprised to find themselves engulfed in heavy fog as they approached the walls of the city. The skies had been clear when they moored the ship, and the air crisp and dry. "Perhaps it is more help from Mount Olympus," said Jason. "It is better that we arrive at the palace unannounced."

Jason and his men thus traveled through the misty streets unobserved. When they arrived at the gates of the palace, the mist dissolved and the palace guards were shocked to see the band of sea-weary heroes standing before them.

"We have traveled far and we come in peace," Jason said to the captain of the guards. "I have some business with your king."

"Then we must prepare a table for you and your men," said the guard, "for the rules of hospitality are strictly observed here in Colchis. You may speak with the king after you have dined at his table and warmed yourself at his hearth. Follow me."

Jason and his men followed the captain into the palace. The captain called out orders, and the palace began to bustle with activity as preparations were made for the guests. Servants lit fires in the hearths and boiled water for baths. Provisions for a great feast were carried up from the cellar, and soon the smell of roasting venison filled the hall. The king's manservants brought silken robes for the Argonauts and took their sea-worn garments away to be mended, then washed and dried by the fires.

Amid all the activity, a little figure darted unobserved among the servants and cooks in the great hall: a tiny child with a golden bow and a quiver of crimson-tipped arrows. The child scampered from one hiding place to another, peeking out at the Argonauts from behind the curtains, searching through the crowd for the king's dark and mysterious daughter. And when finally he saw Medea enter the hall with her sister Chalciope, he squealed with glee and scurried under the banquet table to string his bow. The child was Cupid, the impish son of Aphrodite, sent by his mother as a favor to Hera and Athena. And his arrows carried the joy and pain of love.

Cupid aimed his bow at Medea, and just as the dark-haired sorceress looked upon Jason, he let his arrow fly. The magic arrow pierced Medea's heart, and Cupid scampered away.

Medea suddenly felt faint. She clutched Chalciope's hand.

"Are you all right?" Chalciope asked.

Medea could not speak. She could only nod and continue staring at Jason. The blond warrior in the silken robe was laughing and talking with his men, but Medea didn't see the others; in fact, the rest of the room had become quite a blur to her. She saw only Jason — and he was beautiful and radiant.

All during the great feast Medea sat with her

father and sister, watching Jason. She wondered where he had come from, what his name was, what he had looked like as a boy. When the banquet was almost over, King Aeetes called out for the leader of the Argonauts to come forward and state his business. And when it was Jason who rose to address the king, Medea was afraid her heart would stop.

"We are grateful, sire, for your kindness and hospitality," Jason said. "We are all men of noble birth and have traveled many days and nights from Greece to reach your shores."

King Aeetes looked suspiciously at the table of heroes. "To what end, may we ask?" he said.

"Sire, long ago my kinsman Phrixus was carried from my homeland Iolcus on a golden ram to escape death at the hands of an evil queen. He and his sister Helle flew on the ram's back eastward over the sea, where Helle fell and drowned.

"But the ram delivered Phrixus here to Colchis, and you received him kindly. Since that time, the Fleece of the Golden Ram has been in your possession."

"Yes," said King Aeetes, "the Fleece hangs now in a sacred grove, a gift from your kinsman to repay our generosity. But what is your business with me now?"

"Sire, Phrixus is dead, but the wise men of my

country believe his ghost will not rest until the coat of the golden ram is returned to Greece."

Aeetes glared at Jason, but said nothing.

"Have compassion, sire," Jason said. "We seek only that which is already our own. If the Fleece is returned, we will be at your service to battle your enemies and spread your good name all over Greece. And the gods will surely smile upon you, sire, for we are certain that all of Olympus desires us to take the Golden Fleece home."

King Aeetes' expression had turned to scorn. "So. You've come to *take* from me? That is how you repay my generosity?" Aeetes pounded the table with his fist. "How dare you say the Fleece does not belong to me and my countrymen! We welcomed your kinsman Phrixus when his own family had turned against him!"

Medea held her breath as the young warrior calmly answered her father.

"I am indeed grateful, sire, for the kindness you showed to Phrixus — and to my own men. But hear me, sire; my quest is noble. It is not a plot to steal what belongs to you. I only wish you to return to my kinsmen and countrymen what is rightfully theirs."

King Aeetes looked again at the band of heroes, then glared at Jason. "All right. If your quest is indeed a noble one, sir, and not a plot to steal my lands and my throne; and if, in truth, the gods are helping you, then let them see you through this challenge:

"I have in my fields two bulls with hooves of bronze and breath of fire, and in my chamber, the teeth of the dragon slain by the great Cadmus. This, then, shall be your test. You must yoke the bulls together and use them to plow my field. And in the furrows of this field, you must plant the teeth of the dragon. Once planted, these teeth will grow into a crop of armed warriors, and you must battle them alone.

"If your birth is noble, your cause just, and your quest truly blessed by the gods, this challenge should not prove too great. If you succeed, the Fleece shall be yours."

Medea felt weak. No one could meet such a terrible challenge. The thought of the beautiful young warrior being gored by the bulls or slaughtered in combat with the earthborn men was more than she could bear.

"All right. I accept your challenge," Jason said, and Medea felt her heart would break.

The king glared at Jason for a moment. Then, without another word, he rose from the table and stormed out of the hall.

Medea continued to stare at Jason, hardly aware that her father had gone. Jason returned her gaze and in the moment their eyes met, Medea felt she could see into his very soul. Blushing, she rose abruptly from the table and hurried after her father.

CHAPTER SEVEN

The Bulls

⚓"I've never seen one such as him before," whispered Medea. Dark shadows danced on the temple wall as the young sorceress knelt before the candle-lit altar of Hecate, the moon goddess.

"He's so graceful and strong, and he speaks so beautifully. But when my father said he would have to fight the bulls — " Medea covered her face. "Hecate, tell me what I should do! I cannot betray my father! But I cannot watch Jason be killed! I fear that Cupid must have pierced my heart with his arrow, for I am dying of love for this man! And yet I know I must not love him, for he is my father's enemy! I don't know what to do! Tell me, Hecate!"

The temple was silent. "Aaaah," cried Medea. "Is there no answer? I can no longer think clearly about this . . . I can no longer think at all. . . ."

Medea was about to run from the temple

when she sensed another presence in the room. She turned to look and choked back a scream. For standing before her in the glow of the altar candles was Jason himself.

"I'm sorry," Jason whispered. "I didn't mean to frighten you."

Medea shook her head, unable to speak. Then, fearing this might be an apparition sent by Hecate, she reached out and touched Jason's arm. As soon as she touched him, she knew he was real, and every moment she loved him more.

"Medea, I have come to ask for your help," Jason whispered. "One of Phrixus' grandsons advised me to seek you."

Medea still could not bring herself to speak. She could only stare into Jason's handsome face, into his deep-set blue eyes.

Suddenly Medea heard footsteps on the temple staircase. "My sister," she breathed, and she pulled Jason into the shadows. She could feel his breath on her neck as they stood huddled together waiting for Chalciope to pass; she could feel his heart beating close to her own. When Chalciope had gone, Medea fell to her knees and began to weep.

"What's wrong?" Jason whispered, kneeling beside her.

"I love you!" Medea cried, tears running down

her cheeks. "I love you now, I loved you the first moment I saw you. I don't know who you are, I don't know you at all, but I feel that I would die for love of you. . . ."

"Beautiful princess," Jason said tenderly, "don't let your love bring you sorrow when all it brings me is joy."

"But I can't love you," Medea said. "I love my father, and you are his enemy! I would never betray my father!"

"I hold nothing against your father and wish him no harm," Jason said. "I only want to return to my kinsmen what is rightfully theirs. It is your father who wishes to harm me with his impossible challenge. . . ."

Medea dried her tears. "I fear that what you say is true," she said. "That is why I have prepared this for you." With trembling fingers she reached into the folds of her sorceress' robe and pulled out a small vial. "I did not know whether to give this to you or not. I came to pray for guidance from Hecate; perhaps your presence here is her answer to my prayers." Medea placed the vial in Jason's hand. "Take it quickly," she whispered, "before my conscience makes me change my mind again. . . ."

"What is it?" Jason asked.

"It is a magic ointment made from the blood of Prometheus. Before you go to meet my father's challenge tomorrow, you must rub it over your body and over your shield and helmet. It will protect you and make you invincible for a day, so you need not fear the fiery breath of the bulls nor the swords and spears of the earthborn men. And when the warriors from the earth grow too many in number, you must hurl a stone into their midst. They will turn on one another then, and your task will be done."

"Thank you," said Jason. He touched Medea's cheek and stroked her silky dark hair. "Thank you for saving my life."

"Medea? Are you here?" Medea leaped to her feet when she heard her sister's voice.

"I must go now," she whispered. "Do what I have told you, and you will be safe. And may the gods have pity on a traitorous daughter. . . ."

Medea turned to go, but Jason held her arm. "Wait," he said pulling her close to him. He gazed into her dark eyes for a moment, then kissed her tenderly.

"Medea!" Chalciope called, and Medea slipped from Jason's embrace and rushed away, leaving Jason alone.

. . .

At dawn the next day, all of Colchis made its way to the Plain of Ares. Merchants from the city weaved through the excited crowd selling fruit and wine. Great throngs of spectators scrambled for seats on the hill overlooking the plain as if they were attending a sporting contest.

A royal throne had been prepared for King Aeetes on the hillside, and the crowd roared as he thundered onto the plain in his chariot. The king was clad in full royal battle armor, as if he himself were coming to do combat on the field that day.

Aeetes took his place on the hill with his daughters and his guards; then a hush fell over the crowd as Jason and his men marched boldly onto the plain. The king had ordered that a separate gallery be prepared for the Argonauts, and they took their places in silence, leaving Jason standing alone on the enormous field.

Once again Medea was stunned by the young man's beauty. His blond hair shone like gold, and his tan, muscular body, clad loosely in his leopard skin and oiled with her magic ointment, glistened in the sun.

Jason plunged his spear into the ground, then went to examine the brass yoke and steel plough that were waiting for him in the corner of the field. The magic dragon's teeth hung from the plough's handle in a leather pouch. As Jason bent to strap the pouch over his shoulder, the crowd gasped, then erupted in a thunderous roar. Jason turned in time to see the two vicious bulls charging him, their bronze hooves pounding the earth.

Jason lifted his shield, made magical by Medea's ointment, and held his ground in the path of the onrushing beasts. One by one the raging bulls crashed headlong into the shield, but Jason was unshaken.

The bulls staggered back, stunned by the impact. Bellowing and pawing the ground, they seemed about to charge again; but instead, they breathed forth great columns of fire and engulfed Jason completely in flames.

Aeetes smiled grimly. No mortal could survive the blazing fireball that surrounded the young warrior. But the king's smug satisfaction turned to astonishment as Jason, protected by Medea's magic, stepped from the flames unharmed. And much to Aeetes' displeasure, the crowd started cheering the brave hero on.

Jason spoke gently and soothingly to the two bulls as he prepared their harness. With soft words he forced one and then the other to its knees and into the yoke. Then, throwing his shield over his shoulder, he fastened the great plough to the harness and set to work.

Medea sat by her father and watched with secret

pride as time and again Jason drove the bulls back and forth across the field, churning the earth with the mighty plough. Into each furrow Jason hurled a handful of the dragon's teeth. He worked without stopping, and when at last he had ploughed and sown the last row, it was late in the afternoon.

Jason unleashed the bulls and shooed them away, then took up his spear and helmet. As he turned back to the field, the freshly ploughed earth started to rumble and churn.

Jason watched as a deadly crop of warriors began to spring from the dark furrows. Clad in steel armor, they shot up like corn until there were hundreds of them: a great, inhuman army drawn from the bowels of the earth to battle the single brave hero.

The deadly crop of soldiers shook the dirt from their bodies and drew their swords. As they began to advance on Jason, Medea grew pale with fright. She whispered a special prayer to Hecate and watched as Jason fended off the warriors with his shield, then grabbed a stone from the field.

Jason hurled the stone into the crowd of men. The stone struck one of them in the face, and the warrior reeled, holding his head. Thinking one of his own had struck him, the warrior slashed at the man nearest him with his sword. Then, as Medea had predicted, all the warriors began to turn on each other in great confusion. Ignoring Jason completely, they shouted curses and hacked at each other with their weapons until the field ran red with their blood.

Jason silently watched the gruesome warriors destroy themselves until, finally, only one was left alive. Medea gasped as the last, bloody figure turned viciously on Jason. But in a single, swift move, Jason hurled his spear through the warrior's heart.

The sun sank in a red glow behind the hills, and the crowd watched in stunned silence as Jason pulled his spear from the warrior's body. He wiped his brow, and as the Argonauts and the crowd began to cheer wildly, Jason turned to King Aeetes. His task was done.

CHAPTER EIGHT

The Golden Fleece

❧The great bonfire blazed high into the sky as Castor and Pollux paraded through the camp, carrying Jason on their shoulders. Phrixus' grandsons had brought casks of wine from the city, and a pig was roasting over the open fire. Several of the heroes were taking turns crashing their arms into Jason's invincible shield; others were laughingly helping Orpheus compose a song to honor Jason's victory over the earthborn men. It had been a glorious day, and Jason's triumph was a joyful cause for celebration.

Castor and Pollux carried Jason over to the fire, and, setting him down atop the largest wine cask, they called out to the other men for silence. "It is time for our mighty leader to make a mighty victory speech in honor of his mighty victory today on the mighty plain!" Castor shouted, and all the men laughed.

Jason raised his goblet high above his head. "Thank you, mighty warrior," he said, smiling broadly. "I drink first, as always, to the gods; then to you, my dear friends; and finally, today, to myself. . . ."

Jason bowed to the men and the Argonauts cheered.

"For a field well sown, for a crop well harvested, for a challenge well met, for a quest fulfilled, and . . . for the love of a beautiful woman!"

The Argonauts cheered again, and Pollux bashed a tree against Jason's still-invincible shield. Orpheus struck up a lively tune on his lyre, and soon a great chorus of heroic voices echoed through the woods.

As she ran along the damp wooded path, Medea could hear the singing of the men in the distance and see the sparks of their bonfire flickering above the silhouetted trees. The path was dark and over-grown with brambles. Medea often stumbled; still, she kept running, desperate to reach the man she loved.

Finally Medea came to the clearing and stopped to catch her breath. Her eyes searched the crowd of celebrating heroes for Jason and when she saw him, her heart raced even faster. She closed her eyes and called his name.

"Jason!"

Medea's voice cut through the night, through the crackling of the fire, through the laughter and shouting of the men, through Orpheus' song. And Jason heard his name as if she had whispered it in his ear. He turned from the men and saw her standing at the edge of the clearing, wild and beautiful in the light of the fire.

Jason broke from the group and ran to Medea. He started to embrace her, but she pulled away and began speaking desperately in a terrible, frightened voice. "They're coming, they're coming for you!"

"Who?" said Jason. "Who is coming?"

"My father! My father is wicked and vengeful, and your victory today has only stirred his spirit against you! He swears you shall never have the Golden Fleece, and he has dispatched his soldiers to burn your ship and murder you and your men! Not even my strongest magic is defense against his army! You must go from here, quickly!"

"No! We will not run away! Let them come, and we shall fight them! We shall fight them all!" Jason said. "I would never leave now without the Fleece! It would be better to die!"

Medea fell to her knees and clutched Jason's hands. "Please, please, listen to me!" she begged him. "I fear for my own life as well as yours! I am sure my father recognized my sorcery in your victory today! He could never forgive me, he will kill me, he will kill me. . . ." Medea began to weep. "Flee with me now, Jason. Take me with you!"

"But the Fleece — "

"I can lead you to the Golden Fleece! I can tame the sleepless monster that guards it! We can take the Fleece together, Jason, then leave this awful place! Please, please, I beg you!"

Jason gently pulled Medea to her feet and held her in his arms. "All right," he whispered in her ear. "We will take the Fleece together." Medea looked up. "And I could never leave you here now, even without your father's suspicions." Jason said, "You will come with me to Greece, where we shall be wed, and you shall be my queen. You have my sacred oath."

The two lovers gazed into each other's eyes for a moment, then embraced. Jason called out to the men celebrating by the fire.

"My friends," Jason shouted, "I fear we celebrate too soon. We have been deceived; we must leave here immediately. But we shall not leave without that which is ours. Make haste: Prepare the ship for sailing, but leave the bonfire blazing. The time has come to seize the Golden Fleece!"

• • •

The Argonauts broke camp and boarded the ship. With Medea guiding them, they rowed silently along the twisting Colchis coast until they came to a wooded inlet hidden by tall cypress trees. There they dropped anchor, and Jason followed Medea along a winding path that led from the shore into the forest.

"Why does the sky beyond these woods seem so bright?" Jason asked as they approached a clearing. "Shouldn't the sunrise be to our backs?"

"It is not the sunrise," Medea whispered, pointing. "It is the Fleece. Look."

Jason shielded his eyes and peered through the trees into the clearing. Near the top of the hill grew a huge, gnarled oak — and hanging high in the oak's branches was the dazzling Golden Fleece.

Jason was speechless. He had come to the end of his journey. There was his prize, and it lit the forest like the eastern sun. He began to run across the clearing toward the oak.

"Jason! Wait!" Medea cried. But it was too late. The trunk of the great tree began to move and Jason stopped, horrified. For it was not the trunk of the tree moving at all, but the body of the hideous serpent dragon that guarded the Fleece.

Jason stood frozen with fear as the serpent slithered around the oak. The creature was hideous. When it saw Jason, its eyes glowed fiery red and it opened its huge mouth and let out a hiss that shook the trees. The hiss was the sound of pure evil: the voiceless, wordless, icy sound of all the earth's hatred and cruelty and malice. It chilled Jason's blood.

But as he stared in terror at the horrible hissing dragon, Jason became aware of another sound — a sweet, ethereal, soothing sound. Medea was singing a magical song, an incantation. As she sang, she swayed gently back and forth and started to move closer to the beast.

The serpent looked at Medea for a moment, then began to follow her rhythmic movements with its eyes. The hiss grew softer and less fierce. Soon Medea was standing close enough to touch the creature's great head, and the monster's hiss had grown so soft it was almost a purr.

Medea kept singing, and as she sang she reached slowly into her gown and pulled out two sprigs of freshly cut juniper. Holding a sprig in each hand, she raised her arms above the creature's head.

Medea crushed the juniper sprigs in her fingers as hard as she could. Juniper drops splashed into the monster's fiery eyes. Startled, the serpent bared its yellow fangs and reared up to strike.

Medea jumped back, but the creature did not attack. Her magic had worked; before the serpent could strike, the fiery eyes closed and the awful monster fell to the ground, dead asleep.

Jason raced across the clearing and bounded over the serpent's body. He climbed quickly to the top of the oak, pulled the Fleece from the branches, and leapt to the ground.

Jason ran his fingers through the soft, shining wool, then clutched it to his chest. This was the Golden Fleece, the gleaming coat of the magnificent ram that had borne two children through the sky so many years before. Jason nearly wept, thinking of his ancestors Phrixus and Helle — how they had clung to this same comforting soft wool as the great ram carried them across the heavens.

Jason buried his face in the Fleece for a moment, then raised it high above his head and held it up to the rosy dawn sky, as if offering it to the gods for their approval. It was the hero's moment of glory, and Medea watched with great love as Jason stood triumphant in the shadowy grove, bathed in the light of the Golden Fleece.

· · ·

Nestled in the bow of the *Argo*, Jason held tightly to the Golden Fleece as Medea dozed on his shoulder and the Argonauts rowed swiftly over the open sea.

As the shores of Colchis faded into the shimmering distance, Jason closed his eyes. The waves slapped against the mighty ship, and the fresh, salty air and warm rays of the sun caressed his face. Jason remembered Argus' declaration that a ship such as the *Argo* could never be built. He remembered the temptation to abandon his quest on the island of Lemnos. He remembered his self-doubt after leaving Hercules behind, and his fear when he faced the Clashing Rocks, the fire-breathing bulls, the earth-born warriors, and the sleepless dragon.

Jason knew that a dangerous voyage still lay before him. But for now — for one golden, sunlit moment — he allowed himself to feel deep joy; for he had conquered obstacles both outside himself and *within* himself to succeed in his quest. He had captured the Golden Fleece — and no matter what was to come, that truth would always be with him.